BILLY THE KID

LEGENDS OF THE WEST

BILLY THE KID

Published by Creative Education, 123 South Broad Street, Mankato, Minnesota 56001
Creative Education is an imprint of The Creative Company
Design and Production by EvansDay Design

Photographs by Buffalo Bill Historical Center; Cody, Wyoming; (Vincent Mercaldo Collection; P.71.1983.1, p. 25), Corbis (Craig Aurness, Bettmann, George H. H. Huey, David Muench), Nita Stewart Haley Memorial Library, Midland, Texas

Library of Congress Cataloging-in-Publication Data
Healy, Nick. Billy the Kid / by Nick Healy.
p. cm. — (Legends of the West)
ISBN 1-58341-335-9

1. Billy, the Kid—Juvenile literature. 2. Outlaws—Southwest, New—
Biography—Juvenile literature. 3. Southwest, New—Biography—Juvenile
literature. I. Title. II. Legends of the West (Mankato, Minn.)
F786.B54H43 2005   364.15'52'092—dc22   2004056169

First edition

2 4 6 8 9 7 5 3 1

Cover and page 2 photograph:
Billy the Kid, in the only known photograph of him

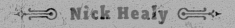 Nick Healy

A TALENT FOR ESCAPE
DEFINED BILLY THE KID'S BRIEF LIFE AND HIS LASTING LEGEND.

DURING HIS DAYS in the American Southwest, he had a knack for finding trouble and evading its consequences. He bolted from jails, fled burning buildings, and eluded hostile outlaws and lawmen alike. But in the end, he could not avoid a violent fate.

When it comes to Billy the Kid, the simplest details prove slippery.

Much said about him—even the name by which he is known—is more fiction than fact. This much is known: His given name was Henry McCarty, and he was a young boy when his family left the slums of New York City. By 1873, they had made their way to New Mexico, then a rough place where settlers were squeezing out the native people.

The Kid came of age in violent and dangerous country. The law was taken lightly; people settled conflicts on their own. Many men lived by a code that said their honor had value above all else. No insult could go unanswered, and life was regarded as an almost trivial thing. In this setting, Henry McCarty turned to crime, and the legend of Billy the Kid was born. Although killed at 21, he lived on in famous tales of the Old West. The truth about him became as difficult to pin down as the man himself.

CHAPTER ONE

The Kid's Troubled Youth

SOME OF THE SIMPLEST FACTS IN
BILLY THE KID'S
LIFE REMAIN MYSTERIOUS.

WHEN WAS HE BORN?
Who were his parents?

Historians who have studied him do not agree, and records from the period are incomplete and unclear. Most likely, he was born in the latter half of 1859 in New York City to a woman named Catherine McCarty. Some historians argue his birth came a year or two later, and a handful question whether New York was his place of birth. However, most evidence points to 1859 as the year of his birth and New York as the place.

He was named Henry McCarty, though he would later use several different names. He had a brother named Joe. Some say the boys' father was a man named Michael McCarty, who died when they were quite young. Others say Catherine McCarty never married the children's father.

Catherine McCarty was born in Ireland, but as a teenager, she fled to America. A terrible famine gripped Ireland in the mid-1840s, when potato crops were blighted across the island nation. While starvation and disease killed thousands of people, many others left in search of a better life in the States. They arrived in their new home with little more than the clothes on their backs and had no choice but to live in impoverished New York neighborhoods. That is where Catherine found herself when she arrived and where she remained when her children were born several years later.

Catherine eventually headed west but stopped short of cowboy country. She and her sons lived for a time in Indianapolis, Indiana, where Catherine told people she was a widow. (Her story supports claims that Billy the Kid was indeed born in New York and was the son of Michael McCarty.) In 1865, she met a man named William Antrim, who became her longtime companion. Along with Antrim, Catherine moved her sons to Wichita, Kansas, where she soon opened a laundry. The boys enjoyed a stable life there for several years, and Henry was known as a spry, sometimes mischievous child. But sudden

European immigrants (like Catherine McCarty) waited in line at Ellis Island's station for a ferry to sweep them into New York City.

William Antrim

Billy the Kid's stepfather never told what he knew about his stepson's life. Perhaps he could have resolved some of the questions about the Kid's birth and his early years. William Antrim had grown up far away in Indiana, where he was born in 1842 and where he eventually met Catherine McCarty. Antrim was her companion for several years before they married. They departed Indiana, along with her two boys, in 1869 and moved to Wichita, Kansas. After Catherine's death in 1874, Antrim had little interest in looking after her sons and left them in the care of others. The boys spent much of their time in boardinghouses while Antrim busied himself with prospecting, hoping to make a fortune in minerals. Near the end of his life, he moved to California, where a niece cared for him until his death in 1922.

changes came when Catherine was diagnosed with a lung disease then called "the consumption." The disease, now known as tuberculosis, can cause terrible coughing and chest pain.

Catherine thought a change in climate might reduce the symptoms of her illness. In 1871, she sold her property in Wichita and moved the family west again, staying briefly in Colorado before settling in New Mexico. Catherine married Antrim on March 1, 1873, in Santa Fe, and 13-year-old Henry was there for the ceremony. The family later headed to a southwestern New Mexico town called Silver City. However, the family's fortunes sank there. Catherine, who found no relief in the New Mexico air, died from tuberculosis on September 16, 1874. Henry and his brother were sent to board with a local family and later bounced in and out of other homes.

A skinny, buck-toothed teenager, Henry hardly seemed destined to become a notorious legend of the West. He enjoyed singing and dancing, and he performed in local shows in Silver City. But he was also known to run with a group of boys who liked to cause trouble. His earliest known crime was stealing a large supply of butter from a local rancher. He quickly sold it and thought he had made an easy profit. But when the rancher reported the butter missing, Henry's guilt was obvious. The sheriff let him off the hook for his first offense. Next time, Henry wouldn't be so lucky.

REWARD

($5,000.00)

Reward for the capture, dead or alive of one Wm. Wright, better known as

"BILLY THE KID"

Age, 18. Height, 5 feet, 3 inches. Weight, 125 lbs. Light hair, blue eyes and even features. He is the leader of the worst band of desperadoes the Territory has ever had to deal with. The above reward will be paid for his capture or positive proof of his death.

JIM DALTON, Sheriff.

DEAD OR ALIVE!

Early in life, Henry was wanted by lawmen, dead or alive; "the Kid" had developed a knack for escaping from jail.

At the very least, Henry was guilty of choosing the wrong friends. While living at a Silver City boardinghouse, he met a man known as Sombrero Jack. His real name was George Shaffer, but his choice of a large Mexican hat won him the nickname. Shaffer broke into a local laundry and stole guns, money, and a bundle of clothing. Then he convinced Henry to hide the clothing for him. When the owner of the boardinghouse discovered the clothes among Henry's things, she turned him in. Sombrero Jack got away while Henry got locked up.

For the first time, Henry demonstrated his uncanny flair for escape. During the night, he shimmied up the jailhouse chimney and climbed onto the roof. He was long gone by the time the sheriff came to check on him in the morning. Henry was still shy of his 16th birthday. His mother had been dead for less than one year. And he was on the run, as he would be for much of his remaining life.

Details from the following two years are scant. Henry fled west into American Indian territory in Arizona. For long stretches of time, his whereabouts and activities are unknown. But it is certain he lived part of that time at the edge of Camp Grant, a U.S. Army outpost not far from the New Mexico border. He seems to have wavered between an honest life and a life of crime. He held jobs, working first on a ranch and later in a small hotel. He also learned how to handle a rifle and a pistol. And he took part in small-time theft and rustling. He often used the name "Henry Antrim" and picked up the nick-name "Kid" because of his boyish appearance. By 1877, he was known to many as Kid Antrim.

Henry's time in Arizona came to a bloody end. He was arrested for horse theft and jailed at Fort Grant. Figuring he was an escape risk, officers at Fort Grant had Henry locked in shackles. The man who fitted the shackles was a blacksmith named Francis Cahill. In the past, Cahill had bullied the much-smaller Henry, and Cahill didn't miss the chance to taunt him in jail. He probably assumed he had nothing to fear from Henry, who would likely be locked away for a good stretch. But Cahill figured wrong. Henry escaped, probably with the help of friends in the military, and on August 17, 1877, the two met again.

A heated argument turned into a wrestling match, and when Cahill pinned him to the ground, Henry managed to draw his pistol and fire into Cahill's stomach. The blacksmith fell limp, and Henry ran away. Cahill lived until the next day, long enough to make a sworn statement naming Henry Antrim as his killer. Henry McCarty, also known as Henry Antrim, also known as the Kid, was on the run again.

The Body Count

If all the stories were true, Billy the Kid might have been the maddest killer in the West. However, many tales about his murderous ways are pure fiction. One well-known story says the Kid was only 12 years old when he first killed another person. As the story goes, a man insulted the Kid's mother on the street, and the Kid responded by stabbing him and running off. No evidence exists to support this story. In fact, the Kid first got into trouble with the law after his mother had died, and his crime was related to a burglary, not a killing. Another common tale says the Kid killed 21 men, one for each year of his short life, and some people claim he killed as many as 40 people. No proof exists to support such numbers. Using reliable evidence, it seems most likely the Kid killed four men on his own and that he was involved in gunfights that claimed the lives of six others.

An Outlaw War

THE KID FEARED HE WOULD BE CHARGED WITH

MURDER IN ARIZONA.

THE SHOOTING OF FRANCIS CAHILL HAD BEEN

declared "criminal and unjustifiable"

BY A CORONER'S JURY.

The Kid might have been able to fight the charge. He could have claimed self-defense. Due to Cahill's superior size and strength, the Kid might have convinced a jury he had no choice but to shoot. But he was not going to risk a trial. He fled Arizona and returned to New Mexico.

The Dolan Gang, which took its leadership from James Dolan (far left), played a bloody role in New Mexico's Lincoln County War.

He had changed in the two years he had been away. He was still a teenager and still looked the part. At 17, he remained short and slim. He would never exceed about 5-foot-8 (1.7 m) in height and roughly 140 pounds (63 kg) in weight. He wore a thin mustache and wispy beard. But the Kid had learned many things while he was away. He could speak fluent Spanish and knew how to handle a gun. He had also gained experience as a ranch hand. Some of his talents, such as stealing horses, were less praiseworthy.

The Kid wanted to stay a step ahead of the law. For a brief time, he stayed with old friends outside Silver City, the town he had fled two years earlier. He worried that Arizona authorities might be looking for him, so he set off for a place where nobody would know him. He also began using a new alias, or assumed name. He called himself "William Bonney." It is not clear where the name came from. It may have had a family connection for Henry, but there is no clear evidence of that. Regardless, William Bonney became the name by which he was widely known. Others shortened the first name to "Billy," and his old nickname—"Kid"—stuck with him. Later, the two merged, and he became "Billy the Kid."

The Kid made his way to Lincoln County in eastern New Mexico. The county was enormous, larger than many eastern states, but its population was small. Much of the land was cattle grazing country. In the tiny town of Lincoln—a

John Tunstall

John Tunstall was an ambitious young man whose dreams of getting rich in the American West cost him his life. Born on March 6, 1853, in London, Tunstall traveled to western Canada when he was 19 years old. His father was a senior partner in an English trading company that gave Tunstall a job in Victoria, British Columbia. He quit the company after three years and headed to California, where he hoped to become a rancher. After a short time there, however, Tunstall decided New Mexico offered more promising opportunities. In 1876, he settled in Lincoln and became a cattle rancher. He believed he could improve his fortunes by entering the retail business in Lincoln, where one general store operated without competition. This move brought Tunstall into conflict with the owner of the existing store, James Dolan. The dispute erupted into violence. Dolan's men shot Tunstall, just 24 years old, outside Lincoln in 1878. The place where he died became known as Tunstall Canyon.

mere handful of buildings scattered along one street—the Kid found honest work. He took a job on a ranch belonging to John Tunstall. An ambitious young Englishman, Tunstall saw opportunities to get rich in Lincoln County. In fact, he sent a letter to family back home saying he hoped to get "half of every dollar that is made in the county by anyone." To do that, he would have to challenge the most powerful businessman in the region, James Dolan.

Dolan's enterprise in Lincoln was known simply as "The House." It was a general store, but it was much more than that. The House sold local ranchers all the supplies they needed. When it came time to sell the cattle, ranchers again had to deal with The House. Dolan, along with his associates, was the only one around who sold cattle to the U.S. government, which needed beef to feed soldiers at a nearby fort and to provide rations to American Indians on a nearby reservation.

By working for Tunstall, the Kid was drawn into serious trouble in Lincoln. Tunstall opened a store to challenge The House, and Dolan and his partners did not take kindly to this. They intended to defeat Tunstall, but they did not intend to do it through honest competition. Dolan believed his honor had been insulted—that Tunstall had failed to show him respect—and he was determined to exact revenge.

Tension in Lincoln grew, and finally, in early 1878, the dispute exploded. One February morning, as Tunstall led a group of horsemen, including the Kid, on a ride from his ranch into Lincoln, they were ambushed by a gang sent by Dolan. When Dolan's men began firing, Tunstall's group scattered. The Kid rode off to find a safe place where he could defend himself, but before he and others could return fire, Tunstall was cornered. The attackers shot Tunstall twice, once in the chest and once in the head. When he fell over dead, the attackers shot his horse as well.

The brutal killing began a long, bloody fight known as the Lincoln County War. This war was not fought by armies but by gangs of hired guns. About 40 or 50 of Tunstall's men banded together to seek revenge. They called themselves the "Regulators," and they were led by Alexander McSween, who had been Tunstall's lawyer. They fought Dolan's men, and the two sides traded sneak attacks and cold-blooded killings. Both groups believed they had the law on their side, and both believed their opponents were criminals.

The Kid was transformed during the Lincoln County War. Witnesses said he was particularly angry after Tunstall's killing. One reported that the Kid looked at his boss's lifeless body and said, "I'll get some of them before I die." The fighting went on for months, and the Kid took part in several violent assaults. He was with a group of Regulators who captured and executed two men they believed had killed Tunstall. He was also with a group that later ambushed Lincoln County

The Kid helped the "Regulators," a gang headed up by Alexander McSween (pictured), wreak havoc in Lincoln County, New Mexico.

sheriff William Brady, who they believed had taken Dolan's side. The Kid and five others hid along Lincoln's main street and cut down Brady in a hail of gunfire that also killed one deputy. The gunfight left the Kid with a bullet wound to his leg, but he managed to escape to safety.

A five-day battle ended the Lincoln County War. By July 19, 1878, Tunstall's men were on the brink of defeat, and a handful of them, including the Kid, were trapped inside McSween's house. Dolan's group had surrounded the house and, after a long standoff, set it on fire. The Kid and a few others planned a risky escape, slipping out a back door and dashing toward safety. As soon as they burst through the smoke, their opponents opened fire. One Regulator was shot; others had to turn back. A lucky few, including the Kid, got out safely. In the end, McSween was dead, the Regulators were defeated, and the Kid was a wanted man.

The Man in the Picture

O nly one photograph of the Kid is known to exist. It is an early kind of photo known as a tintype. The picture has been copied many times, and reprints are often blurry and marred. Many conclusions about the Kid are based on this single photograph, and they may be incorrect. For example, many people say he was left-handed because the photo shows him holding a gun with his left hand. One movie made about him was even called *The Left-Handed Gun*. However, in a tintype photo, the image is reversed, meaning he actually held the gun in his right hand. Also, some observers have sized up the Kid's appearance based on the tintype. They say he was short, chubby, and homely. However, people who saw the Kid in real life reported different opinions. The *Las Vegas Gazette* described him as "a quite handsome looking fellow" who "looked and acted a mere boy."

CHAPTER THREE

❧ A Wanted Man ❧

THE LINCOLN COUNTY WAR WAS OVER, BUT
THE KID'S TROUBLES
WERE JUST BEGINNING. DURING THE DISPUTE,
men on both sides had been
INDICTED FOR MURDER.

That meant they could be brought to trial on criminal charges carrying a penalty of death. Several men were accused in the Tunstall killing that set off the fighting. They included Dolan himself, who was charged as an accessory to murder. Several Regulators also faced charges. The Kid and two others were indicted for shooting Sheriff Brady. To put the troubles in Lincoln County to rest, and to try to return the area to normal, the governor of New Mexico issued a "general pardon" to both sides. However, the pardon excluded anyone who was already under indictment. As a result, the Kid still had to dodge the law.

✦ ✦ ✦ ✦ ✦ ✦ ✦ ✦ ☞

In this engraving, Billy the Kid shoots down a foe in a saloon. As the bloody Lincoln County War raged on, the Kid's legend grew.

Along with a small group of remaining Regulators, the Kid roamed the countryside. They were angry about McSween's death and wanted revenge, but there was little they could do about it. The Kid returned to the sort of crimes he had committed before the war. He and his companions stole horses and cattle, and they gambled. The Kid was very skilled at a card game called monte, and he often claimed he made his living as a gambler. Late in 1878, after months of drifting about in New Mexico and Texas, he decided to return to Lincoln. He went with some hope that he could make things right and go on with his life.

Although the murder indictment hovered over him, the Kid had little reason to believe he would be arrested. The local sheriff's department was in disarray, and many feared arresting a Regulator like the Kid would only reignite the violence. Tensions remained high between Dolan's group and those who had stood with McSween. Surprisingly, the Kid wound up helping to structure a strange treaty between the two sides. They agreed they would no longer fight each other and would not testify against each other.

The men celebrated the new peace by getting drunk—all of them except the Kid. He was not a regular drinker, so he remained a sober witness to what happened when the drunken mob spilled into the street. The men stopped an innocent passerby, a lawyer named Huston Chapman. One of the men drew

Pat Garrett

He is remembered as the man who shot Billy the Kid, but Pat Garrett's time as Lincoln County sheriff was only one chapter in an interesting life. Born in 1850, he grew up on a Louisiana cotton plantation. After both of Garrett's parents died when he was still a teenager, he moved to Texas, where he worked as a trail driver and buffalo hunter. His first wife died, and Garrett married Apolonaria Gutierres in 1880, months before being elected sheriff of Lincoln County. He and his wife had eight children. After ending the criminal career of Billy the Kid, Garrett experienced twists and turns. He gained fame for killing the Kid, but he lost when he ran for sheriff of newly created Chaves County. He later moved to Texas and back to New Mexico, where he became sheriff of Dona Ana County. He was shot and killed in 1908 while traveling in New Mexico.

his gun and ordered the lawyer to dance. Unwilling to be made a fool, Chapman refused, and after an argument, Chapman was shot in the chest. The men continued their celebration and left the dead man lying in the street.

Chapman's murder caused a ripple of fear in Lincoln, exactly what the new governor of the territory did not want. Lew Wallace had been appointed by President Rutherford B. Hayes to clean up the lawless mess in New Mexico. Wallace had declared the general pardon after the Lincoln County War and appointed new law officers to restore order. He needed to bring Chapman's killers to justice, or he would risk losing the public's confidence and support. The Kid then made a shrewd move. He offered to tell everything he had seen and testify against Chapman's killers. In return, he asked that the governor let him off the hook for his crimes during the war. Wallace took the deal.

The Kid kept his end of the bargain. He allowed himself to be arrested in Lincoln and gave his testimony, just as he and the governor had agreed. The Kid waited for the governor to wipe away the indictments against him, but the governor took no action. Growing impatient, the Kid walked away from jail and rode out of Lincoln in June 1879. The local sheriff did nothing to stop him. For more than a year, the Kid returned to his old tricks, moving from town to town, dancing, gambling, and committing a variety of crimes. The Kid still hoped the governor would honor the deal, though it seemed unlikely. The next year, a new sheriff was elected in Lincoln County, and he promised to round up outlaws like the Kid. A former buffalo hunter, Sheriff Pat Garrett, a tall and intimidating figure, vowed to restore law and order in Lincoln County.

Catching the Kid did not prove easy, but in late December 1880, Garrett tracked him and four other outlaws to an abandoned house near Stinking Springs. When one of the men stepped out of the house at dawn to feed the horses, Garrett and his deputies fired. They thought they had killed the Kid, but it turned out to be one of his friends. After a short standoff, the men inside the house surrendered. Having been labeled by newspapers as New Mexico's number-one outlaw, the Kid would finally stand trial.

The charge of murder carried a penalty of death, but the Kid remained upbeat. While being transported for trial, he spoke cheerfully with a reporter. "What's the use of looking on the gloomy side? I guess the laugh's on me this time," he said. But his sunny outlook could not help him in a Mesilla, New Mexico, courtroom. In 1881, he was tried for the murder of Sheriff William Brady, and a jury found him guilty. He was sentenced to hang and sent back to Lincoln County to await his execution.

In Lincoln, the site of his greatest glories and worst crimes, the Kid had one more card to play. In the past, the county had

This illustration depicts Sheriff Pat Garrett bringing Billy the Kid and his gang in to jail. The Kid escaped one last time, but not for long.

never had a properly secure jail; prisoners were merely stuffed away in the cellar beneath the sheriff's office. But things had changed since the Kid last rode out of town. The large building that had once been The House, Dolan's store and offices, was now the courthouse and jail. Garrett locked the Kid in a room next to the sheriff's office and left two guards to watch him. On the night of April 28, 1881, the Kid attempted an escape.

His plan was simple and brutal. He asked one guard to take him to the privy behind the courthouse, and on the way back, he attacked the guard and wrestled away his gun. When the man ran for help, the Kid shot him. Then he grabbed a shotgun from the sheriff's office, leaned out a window, and took aim at the second guard, who was in the courtyard. With both guards dead, the Kid climbed out onto the balcony and spoke to a small crowd gathering in front of the building. He said that anyone who interfered with his escape would share the guards' fate; the onlookers stood by and did nothing as the Kid jumped on a stolen horse and rode out of town. It would be his last taste of freedom.

The Kid's Letters

Some accounts of Billy the Kid's life report that he received no schooling and could not read or write. While it is unlikely he received a great deal of formal schooling as a child, he was not illiterate. In fact, he was known to be an avid reader of *Police Gazette*, a magazine that featured thrilling stories of criminals and cops. In fact, some historians believe those stories may have inspired the Kid by making the outlaw life seem glamorous. He could also write, and some of his letters were stored in the records of Governor Lew Wallace. In one letter, the Kid reminded the governor of a deal between them. He hoped the governor would let him off the hook for misdeeds during the Lincoln County War. "I expect that you have forgotten what you promised me ... but I have not," the Kid wrote. "I have done everything that I promised you I would, and you have done nothing that you promised me."

CHAPTER FOUR

Violent Death Builds a Legend

SHERIFF GARRETT HEARD ABOUT
THE ESCAPE
THE FOLLOWING DAY
and soon began searching
FOR THE OUTLAW.

Two and a half months later, he tracked him to Fort Sumner, an old military post northeast of Lincoln. On the night of July 14, 1881, the Kid walked into a darkened room, where Garrett was waiting for him. The sheriff fired twice, and the outlaw fell dead. He was 21 years old.

The Kid made an unlikely legend. During much of his short life, he was merely a small-time crook. He bounced around the Southwest, often falling under the influence of more powerful people and fighting other people's battles. Even during the Lincoln County War, he remained a face in the crowd, not a leader of his gang. But toward the end of his life, he suddenly emerged as a famous villain. Many of the men who once led the Regulators had either been killed or had left New Mexico, but the Kid remained. He had been on the losing side in Lincoln County, and in the aftermath, his group received the blame for the fear and violence that gripped the region.

His fame, or infamy, had roots in the newspapers of the time. After the Lincoln County War, New Mexico papers described the continued lawlessness of the area, and the Kid became a focus of their reporting. After all, he was known to have ambushed the sheriff of Lincoln County. He had been indicted for murder but not yet brought to trial. He continued to drift around with the remaining Regulators, to steal horses, and to generally ignore the law. In 1880, the *Las Vegas* (N.M.) *Gazette* described a "gang of outlaws" that was "terrorizing the people of Fort Sumner and vicinity." The article said the gang fell "under the leadership of 'Billy the Kid,' a desperate cuss." Other papers across the country picked up on the story. He was no longer a crook called the Kid by his acquaintances; he was a bandit known far and wide as Billy the Kid.

Standing tall and taking no bull in his effort to clean up Lincoln County, new sheriff Pat Garrett hunted down and killed the Kid.

Governor Lew Wallace

Lew Wallace was a famous man in 19th-century America, but his notoriety had little to do with Billy the Kid. Wallace was born in Indiana in 1827. He worked as a newspaper reporter after college and later attended law school. After becoming a lawyer, he won a seat in the state senate. From the outset of the Civil War, Wallace served in the Union Army, achieving the rank of major general. But he didn't make his name in politics or in the military. Literature was his ticket to fame and fortune. Wallace published a novel called *The Fair God* in 1873, and during his time as New Mexico governor, he worked on his second book. The book was called *Ben-Hur*, and it became enormously popular. Within a few years of its publication, Wallace was able to retire to Indiana and devote his life to writing. He died in 1905. Movie versions of *Ben-Hur* were first made during the silent-film era, and a 1959 version became a legendary epic and box-office hit.

The newspapers closely detailed the closing chapters of his life. After his surrender to Garrett, the *Gazette* described the scene when he was paraded into town, chained to another prisoner. The Kid enjoyed the attention, and his attitude only increased his notoriety. "There was a big crowd gazing at me, wasn't there?" he asked a reporter. "Well, perhaps some of them will think me half a man now; everyone seems to think I was some kind of animal." Newspapers followed his trial and sentence to hang, and his spectacular escape brought an explosion of attention. Reporters described him as a "young demon" and "murderer from infancy," but they also noted "his coolness and steadiness of nerve in executing his plan."

Headlines celebrated the death of the Kid when Garrett at last got his man. The final moments of the Kid's life came in a confused scene at the home of his friend Pete Maxwell. Garrett had ducked into Maxwell's darkened bedroom to ask if the Kid was staying there. Moments later, the Kid stepped into the room. He realized someone other than his friend was there, but he couldn't see Garrett's face. The last thing the Kid said was "*Quien es?*" (Spanish for "Who is it?"). Garrett fired twice into the blackness, and the event made news around the country. Far away in the East, the *New York Sun* reported, "His death is hailed with great joy."

Garrett himself may be responsible for the lasting fame of Billy the Kid. With the help of a man named Ash Upson, Garrett

Actor Paul Newman portrayed Billy the Kid as a dashing young daredevil in the film The Left-Handed Gun *in 1958.*

created a book that claimed to tell the Kid's life story. Upson was a failed journalist who worked as a postmaster in New Mexico. They called their book *The Authentic Life of Billy the Kid*, though much of its contents did not match reality. The book, published less than one year after the Kid's death, includes Garrett's version of events after he became Lincoln County's sheriff. The rest of the book—describing the Kid's childhood and his life before the Lincoln County War—was mostly a tall tale.

An image of Billy the Kid emerged from Upson and Garrett's book. In the late 1800s, cheap novels portrayed Billy the Kid as a vicious, blood-thirsty killer who could hide behind a cheery smile. As decades passed, he seemed to fade from attention, but renewed interest came in the 1920s. A popular book called *The Saga of Billy the Kid* created a new image for the old outlaw. The book, written by Walter Noble Burns, portrayed him as a heroic figure. Burns wrote about a bandit who, like Robin Hood, stuck up for the poor and disadvantaged, and committed crimes to protect or benefit them. Billy the Kid's image drifted farther from the reality of his life.

The truth was left behind entirely when Hollywood discovered Billy the Kid. More than 40 movies have been made about him. Famous actors such as Val Kilmer, Paul Newman, and Roy Rogers have portrayed him on the big screen, and many films have created new personalities for the young man behind the name. In some films, he is an avenger who acts only because he or his friends have been wronged. In others, he is an unpredictable monster who kills for sport. In one movie, he is a hero who receives thanks from a little girl for making her town safe. Most recently, the movies *Young Guns* and *Young Guns II* portrayed Billy the Kid as a handsome teenager with a short temper.

Though so much has been said and written about Billy the Kid, he remains a mysterious figure. Some people claim he did not die in 1881, and that Pat Garrett shot another man. They say he escaped, and that he lived out his life under a different name. Most historians do not take these stories seriously, and solid evidence says they are not true. Still, the controversy seems fitting for Henry McCarty, the boy who became known as Billy the Kid. His short life was marked by his knack for unlikely escapes, and more than 120 years after his death, the truth about him remains elusive.

Did the Kid Survive?

Some people claim Pat Garrett shot another man that day in 1881 and that Billy the Kid escaped. Some people say the Kid later lived under the name "John Miller" and ran a cattle ranch in western New Mexico. Others believe the story of a Texas man named Brushy Bill Roberts, who before his death in 1950 claimed he was Billy the Kid. There is no good evidence to support these claims, yet the issue has not been put to rest. In 2004, New Mexico officials considered a request to exhume the bodies of Billy the Kid and his mother. Supporters of the plan hoped they could use DNA to prove the man buried at Fort Sumner was the real Billy the Kid. But even that plan had serious problems. The cemetery where Catherine McCarty was buried was moved several years after her death. There was no way to know that each casket was carefully reburied and marked with the proper headstone. Her grave marker could easily have ended up over someone else's body.

Further Information

BOOKS

Marrin, Albert. *Cowboys, Indians, and Gunfighters*.
New York: Atheneum, 1993.

Thrasher, Thomas. *Gunfighters of the American West*.
San Diego: Lucent Books, 2000.

Walker, Dale L. *Legends and Lies*. New York: Forge, 1997.

FILMS

Gold Rush and Gun Fights. 1997. 50 min. Goldhil Video.

Gunfighters of the Old West. 1992. 73 min. Dan Dalton Productions.

Young Guns II. 1990. 105 min. Fox Video.

WEB SITES

Billy the Kid Historic Preservation Society
http://www.aboutbillythekid.com

Historical Society of New Mexico
http://www.hsnm.org

National Association for Outlaw and Lawman History
http://www.outlawlawman.com

Index

A

Antrim, William (stepfather) 8, 10, 11

B

Billy the Kid (Henry McCarty, Henry Antrim,
     William Bonney)
  birth 7
  childhood 8, 10, 11
  dancing 11, 31
  death 30, 37, 41, 45
  escape from "The House" 34, 41
  first arrest and jailing 13
  first escape 13
  gambling 29, 31
  killings 14, 15, 22, 34
  murder trial 32, 41
  newspaper reports about 38, 41
  physical description 11, 19, 25, 43
  post-death legend 38, 41, 43
  tintype photo of 25
books 41, 43
  Authentic Life of Billy the Kid, The 43
  Saga of Billy the Kid, The 43
Brady, William 24, 27, 32
Burns, Walter Noble 43

C

Cahill, Francis 14, 17
Chapman, Huston 29, 31

D

Dolan, James 20, 21, 22, 24, 27, 29, 34

F

Fort Sumner 37, 38, 45

G

Garrett, Pat 30, 32, 34, 37, 41, 43, 44, 45

H

Hayes, Rutherford B. 31

I

Indianapolis, Indiana 8, 10
Ireland 8

L

Lincoln County War 21, 22, 24, 27, 31, 35, 38, 43
Lincoln, New Mexico 19, 20, 21, 29, 31, 32

M

Maxwell, Pete 41
McCarty, Catherine (mother) 7, 8, 10, 11, 45
McCarty, Joe (brother) 8
McCarty, Michael (father) 8
McSween, Alexander 22, 24, 29
movies 25, 43, 44
  Left-Handed Gun, The 25
  Young Guns 44
  Young Guns II 44

N

New Mexico 11, 13, 17, 29, 30, 31, 32, 38, 43
New York, New York 5, 7, 8

R

"Regulators" 22, 24, 27, 29, 38

S

Shaffer, George ("Sombrero Jack") 13
Silver City, New Mexico 11, 13, 19
Stinking Springs, New Mexico 32

T

Tunstall Canyon 20
Tunstall, John 20, 21, 22, 24, 27

U

Upson, Ash 41, 43

W

Wallace, Lew 31, 35, 40
Wichita, Kansas 8, 10, 11